MW01233086

I'm Reading About

DONALD TRUMP

by Carole Marsh

Donald J. Trump is the 45th President of the United States.

How much do you know about America's newest leader?

Let's start reading and learn!

Donald J. Trump was born in New York City, New York.
He was born on June 14, 1946.
Donald was the fourth of five children—
three boys and two girls.

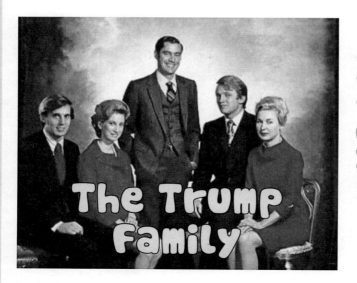

The Trump Family

New York
became a state
in 1788.

SCHOOL DAYS

When he was 13 years old, Donald
began attending the New York Military Academy.

The classes were hard!
The military training was hard!
But Donald did well, and became a class leader.

Donald played on sports teams
at the academy:
baseball, football, and soccer!

New York Military Academy

1889

Donald Trump

Donald Trump attended the University of Pennsylvania. It is a very old and respected college. Benjamin Franklin founded the university before the American Revolution!

Donald specialized in business classes. He studied subjects like accounting and marketing. He learned how to run a business!

business: the activity of making, buying, and selling goods or services

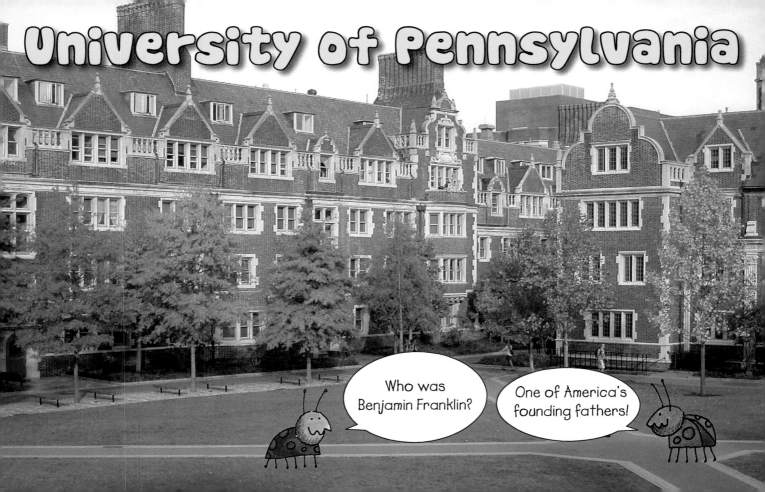

After college, Donald Trump went to work!
He worked for his father's real estate business.
It was named Elizabeth Trump and Son.
Donald's grandmother Elizabeth started the company!

Mr. Trump's family business built houses.
The houses were located in the New York City
boroughs of Brooklyn, Queens, and Staten Island.
The company was very successful!

The five boroughs of New York City
are sections of the larger city.

Elizabeth Trump

I love New York!

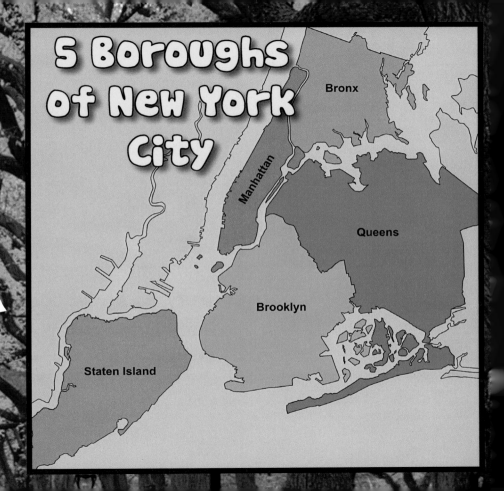

5 Boroughs of New York City

Bronx

Manhattan

Queens

Brooklyn

Staten Island

HOTELS

Soon, Donald Trump took over the family business.
He renamed it The Trump Organization.
Mr. Trump began to build beautiful hotels and other
buildings in New York City.

One of his most famous buildings is Trump Tower!
The luxurious skyscraper is 58 stories high.
It includes apartments, stores, offices, and
an indoor waterfall!

Famous Skyscraper

TRUMP TOWER

Mr. Trump continued to expand his business!
Besides hotels, he built gambling casinos,
resorts, and golf courses.

The Trump properties are luxurious places
for people to relax and have fun.
They were created to be beautiful and inviting!

I want to learn to play golf.

But you don't have any hands!

Resorts & Sports

Taj Mahal Hotel & Casino

Trump International Beach Resort

Trump National Doral Golf Club

The Trump Organization is involved in many other businesses besides real estate.
In fact, the company has about 500 businesses!

Here are just a few examples:

⭐ Donald J. Trump Signature Collection
   Dress shirts and ties

⭐ Trump Productions, LLC
   TV production company

⭐ Trump Model Management
   Modeling agency

More Businesses

FAMILY

Mrs. Melania Trump

Don Jr.

Ivanka

Donald Trump's family!

Eric

Tiffany

Barron

Melania Trump

Arctic Ocean

Atlantic Ocean

Baltic

EUROPE

SLOVENIA

Black Sea

Mediterranean Sea

800 mi

Melania Trump is from the European country of Slovenia.
She became an American citizen in 2006.
Melania is a woman of many accomplishments:

⭐ Studied architecture and design in college

⭐ Was a highly successful fashion model

⭐ Has her own line of jewelry and skincare products

⭐ Speaks five languages

Slovenia became an independent state in 1991. It used to be part of Yugoslavia.

MELANIA

Books and TV

Apprentice

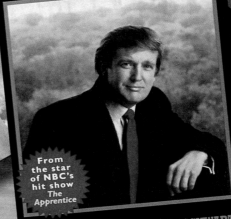

#1 NATIONAL BESTSELLER

TRUMP
THE ART OF THE DEAL

From the star of NBC's hit show *The Apprentice*

DONALD J. TRUMP with **TONY SCHWARTZ**

Donald Trump enjoyed advising others
on how to succeed in business.
He has written more than 15 books!
The most well known is *The Art of the Deal*.

Mr. Trump also hosted two TV shows!
In *The Apprentice*, contestants competed for a job.
A few years later, he launched
The Celebrity Apprentice.
In that show, famous people competed to win money
for charity!

What are the worst words to hear on *The Celebrity Apprentice*?

You're fired!

Trump's Slogan

On June 16, 2015, Donald Trump announced that he was running for President of the United States!
That was a very unusual announcement because businessmen typically do not run for political office.

But Mr. Trump decided he wanted to make a difference.
He said it was time for change in America.
He said he wanted to "Make America Great Again"!

Campaign Mode

Through 2015 and much of 2016,
Mr. Trump ran against up to 16 other candidates
from the Republican Party!
They competed in primary elections around the U.S.

Because he is a billionaire, Donald Trump
traveled in style.
He flew from state to state in his own airplane!

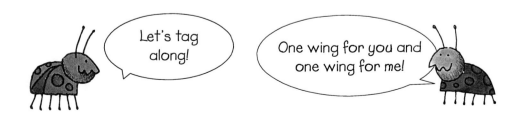

PRIMARIES

Mike Pence

Donald Trump won enough votes to become
the Republican Party nominee for U.S. President!
He chose Indiana governor Mike Pence
to be his running mate.

The candidates criss-crossed the country.
Thousands of people attended their rallies.
Very often, there was not enough room at the rallies
for all the people who wanted to attend!

During the campaign, Mr. Trump
loved to use Twitter!

Donald Trump ran against Democratic candidate
Hillary Clinton for President of the United States.

Mrs. Clinton was a very strong opponent!
She had served as First Lady, a U.S. Senator,
and U.S. Secretary of State.

The two candidates made speeches,
gave countless interviews, and
participated in televised debates.
They traveled across America!

I'm exhausted
just thinking
about it!

THE ELECTION

When the American people voted,
Donald J. Trump was elected as the
45th President of the United States!

It was a hard-fought and historic election.
In the end, the American people put their trust
in Donald Trump to guide the country!

President Trump won 30
out of the 50 states.

NEW PRESIDENT

The Businessman President

Read more fascinating facts about President Trump:

⭐ He has eight grandchildren.
⭐ His nickname is "The Donald."
⭐ His three oldest children run his business empire.
⭐ He relaxes by playing golf, often with his son Barron.
⭐ He enjoys hamburgers, Diet Coke,
and cherry–vanilla ice cream!

Glad to meet you, Mr. President!

I think he means business!

GLOSSARY

apprentice: a person who works for another in order to learn a trade or skill

architecture: the art or science of designing and creating buildings

debate: discussion where people talk about opposite sides of a specific subject or subjects

luxurious: extremely comfortable, elegant, or enjoyable

primary election: an election that narrows the field of candidates before an election for office

rally: mass meeting of people showing support for a cause

real estate: property consisting of land or buildings

running mate: the candidate for vice president in a U.S. presidential election